I Am Fair

by Melissa Higgins

Consulting Editor: Gail Saunders-Smith, PhD

Content Consultant: Susan M. Swearer, PhD
Professor of School Psychology and Licensed
Psychologist; Co-Director, Bullying Research Network
University of Nebraska–Lincoln

CAPSTONE PRESS
a capstone imprint

Pebble Books are published by Capstone Press,
1710 Roe Crest Drive, North Mankato, Minnesota 56003
www.capstonepub.com

Library of Congress Cataloging-in-Publication Data
Higgins, Melissa, 1953–
I am fair / by Melissa Higgins.
pages cm.—(Pebble books. I don't bully)
Summary: "Simple text and full color photographs describe how to be fair,
not a bully"—Provided by publisher.
Includes bibliographical references and index.
Audience: Age 5–8.
Audience: K to grade 3.
ISBN 978-1-4765-4069-6 (library binding)
ISBN 978-1-4765-5173-9 (paperback)
ISBN 978-1-4765-6038-0 (ebook pdf)
1. Fairness—Juvenile literature. I. Title.
BJ1533.F2H54 2014
179'.9—dc23   2013029995

Note to Parents and Teachers
The I Don't Bully set supports national curriculum standards
for social studies related to people and cultures. This book
describes being fair. The images support early readers
in understanding the text. The repetition of words and
phrases helps early readers learn new words. This book also
introduces early readers to subject-specific vocabulary words,
which are defined in the Glossary section. Early readers may
need assistance to read some words and to use the Table of
Contents, Glossary, Read More, Internet Sites, and Index
sections of the book.

Table of Contents

I Play by the Rules

I treat everyone
the same way.
I'm fair.
I don't bully!

I play by the rules.
Kids who bully only care
about winning.

I wait and take my turn.
Kids who bully push
others out of the way.

I share with everyone.
Kids who bully
leave others out.

**I Am
Open Minded**

I see different sides
of a problem. Kids who
bully don't think about
other people's feelings.

I listen to everyone.
Kids who bully
don't care what others
have to say.

I Treat People the Same

I try to treat everyone in the same way. Kids who bully pick favorites.

If a bully is being
unfair to me,
I stand up for myself.

Everyone Deserves a Chance

Being fair means everyone can play and be heard. No one deserves to be bullied!

Glossary

bully—to be mean to someone else over and over again

deserve—to have a right to something

equally—in the same way

fair—in an equal way

Read More

Marsico, Katie. *Taking Turns!* Kids Can Make Manners Count. Ann Arbor, Mich.: Cherry Lake Pub., 2013.

Pryor, Kimberley Jane. *Fairness.* Values. New York: Marshall Cavendish Benchmark, 2011.

Williams, Sam. *Sharing.* Little World Social Skills. Vero Beach, Fla.: Rourke Educational Media, 2013.

Internet Sites

FactHound offers a safe, fun way to find Internet sites related to this book. All of the sites on FactHound have been researched by our staff.

Here's all you do:

Visit *www.facthound.com*

Type in this code: 9781476540696

Check out projects, games and lots more at
www.capstonekids.com

Index

Word Count: 120
Grade: 1
Early-Intervention Level: 12

Editorial Credits
Jeni Wittrock, editor; Juliette Peters, designer; Svetlana Zhurkin, media
researcher; Kathy McColley, production specialist; Sarah Schuette, photo stylist;
Marcy Morin, photo scheduler

Photo Credits
Capstone Studio: Karon Dubke, cover, 4, 6, 10, 14, 20; Shutterstock:
bikeriderlondon, 12, michaeljung, 18, Monkey Business Images, 8, 16